PUBLIC LIBRARY, DISTRICT OF COLUMBIA

D1538962

PUBLIC LIBRARY DISTRICT OF COLUMBIA

Sports and Activities

Let's Play Basketball!

by Carol K. Lindeen

Consulting Editor: Gail Saunders-Smith, PhD

5180 **Consultant:** Kymm Ballard, MA 7576
Physical Education, Athletics, and Sports Medicine Consultant
North Carolina Department of Public Instruction

Capstone press

Mankato, Minnesota

Pebble Plus is published by Capstone Press,
151 Good Counsel Drive, P.O. Box 669, Mankato, Minnesota 56002.
www.capstonepress.com

Copyright © 2006 by Capstone Press. All rights reserved.
No part of this publication may be reproduced in whole or in part, or stored in a retrieval system, or
transmitted in any form or by any means, electronic, mechanical, photocopying, recording, or otherwise,
without written permission of the publisher. For information regarding permission, write to Capstone Press,
151 Good Counsel Drive, P.O. Box 669, Dept. R, Mankato, Minnesota 56002.
Printed in the United States of America

1 2 3 4 5 6 11 10 09 08 07 06

Library of Congress Cataloging-in-Publication Data
Lindeen, Carol K., 1976–
    Let's play basketball! / by Carol K. Lindeen.
    p. cm. — (Pebble plus. Sports and activities)
    Includes bibliographical references and index.
    ISBN-13: 978-0-7368-5362-0 (hardcover)
    ISBN-10: 0-7368-5362-6 (hardcover)
    1. Basketball—Juvenile literature. I. Title. II. Series.
GV885.1.L494 2006
796.323—dc22   2005017943

Summary: Simple text and photographs present the skills, equipment, and safety concerns of basketball.

Editorial Credits
Heather Adamson, editor; Kia Adams, designer; Kelly Garvin, photo researcher

Photo Credits
All photos Capstone Press/Karon Dubke except page 13, Shutterstock/Klementiev Alexey

Note to Parents and Teachers

The Sports and Activities set supports national physical education standards related
to recognizing movement forms and exhibiting a physically active lifestyle. This book
describes and illustrates basketball. The images support early readers in understanding
the text. The repetition of words and phrases helps early readers learn new words.
This book also introduces early readers to subject-specific vocabulary words, which are
defined in the Glossary section. Early readers may need assistance to read some words
and to use the Table of Contents, Glossary, Read More, Internet Sites, and Index sections
of the book.

Table of Contents

Playing Basketball

Pass, shoot, swish!

Basketball players play

as a team.

Basketball players dribble
the ball as they run.
They throw and catch.
They pass the ball.

Basketball players jump.

They try to get by

the other players.

They shoot the ball

into the hoop.

Players score points

for making baskets.

Baskets count for one, two,

or three points.

Equipment

Basketballs are easy
to bounce and catch.
They are made of rubber
and covered
with bumpy grips.

Basketball hoops have
a backboard and a net.
Hoops are at the ends
of flat courts.

Safety

Basketball players guard each other carefully. They try not to push or shove.

Basketball players rest.
They drink water and wait
for their turn to play.

Having Fun

Dribble, pass, jump,
and shoot.
Let's play basketball!

Glossary

basket—a score made in basketball when a player throws the basketball through the hoop; baskets can be worth 1, 2, or 3 points.

court—a flat space for playing a ball game; a basketball court is shaped like a rectangle with one basket at each end.

dribble—to bounce the ball with one hand while moving down the court

guard—to use your arms and body to try to keep a player on the other team from getting the ball or shooting; basketball players cannot push, grab, or trip players they guard.

hoop—a round ring on a backboard; a basketball hoop is a metal circle with a net hanging from it.

pass—to bounce or throw the ball to another person on the same team

shoot—to throw or toss the basketball toward the hoop

Read More

Eule, Brian. *Basketball for Fun!* Sports for Fun! Minneapolis: Compass Point Books, 2003.

Fauchald, Nick. *Jump Ball! You Can Play Basketball.* Game Day. Minneapolis: Picture Window Books, 2004.

Klingel, Cynthia Fitterer and Robert B. Noyed. *Basketball.* Wonder Books. Chanhassen, Minn.: Child's World, 2001.

Internet Sites

FactHound offers a safe, fun way to find Internet sites related to this book. All of the sites on FactHound have been researched by our staff.

Here's how:

1. Visit *www.facthound.com*

2. Type in this special code **0736853626** for age-appropriate sites. Or enter a search word related to this book for a more general search.

3. Click on the **Fetch It** button.

FactHound will fetch the best sites for you!

Index

Word Count: 124
Grade: 1
Early-Intervention Level: 13

FGR

JUV

796.32

LIN

c.1

11/3/06